CW01314583

This book belongs to

....

To Belle and Lana,
my inspiration for this book,
and Rhiannon for her continued support.

Materials we often recycle

Glass

Metals

Plastics

Paper & Card

Plastics, metals, card and glass are useful and all around. But, did you know, when they're thrown away they end up in the ground?

Lots of rubbish made from these will never rot away. So, a bottle thrown away years ago is still there to this day!

Our rubbish is taken to landfill, and pushed into deep holes. Stopping recyclables going here is now the real goal.

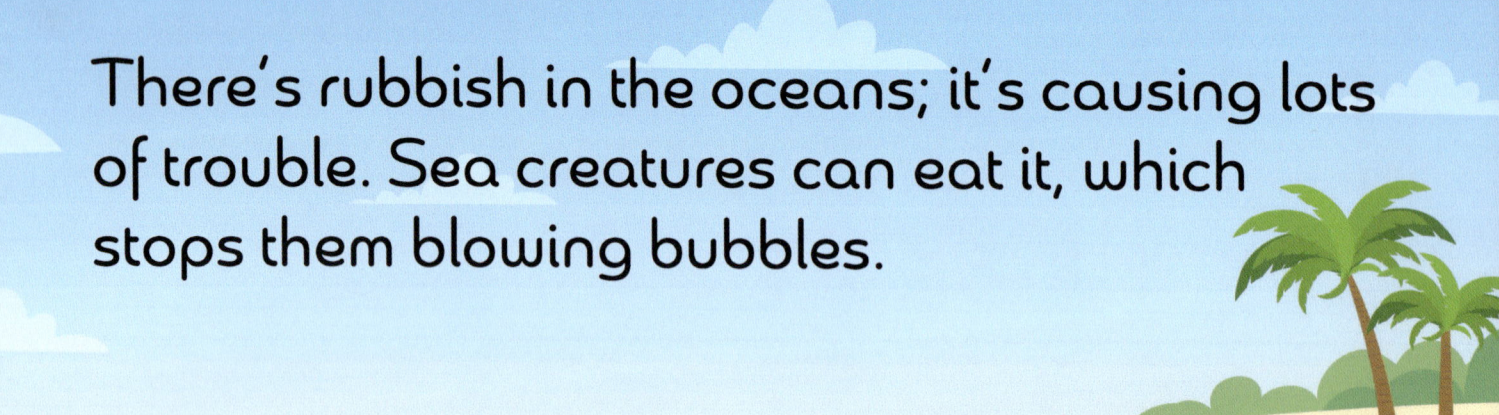

There's rubbish in the oceans; it's causing lots of trouble. Sea creatures can eat it, which stops them blowing bubbles.

It's washed onto our beaches, which is pretty yucky. If you saw no rubbish on holiday, you'd be very lucky!

There are lots of people helping to make this problem go away. They're changing the way we recycle and making it clear as day.

Even though you are small and the world is pretty large, if everyone made the effort, we would all soon lead the charge.

Recycling can be simple – it just takes a little thought. So it's OK to stop and think where to put your plastic fork.

Recycling is amazing – rubbish is made into other things. It's like a superhero changing shape, if we just use the right bins.

If you're ever unsure what to do, go and ask a grown-up. They will show you the right bin so our landfills don't fill up.

Our world is a very special place; caring for it can be fun. Let's all start making changes so it's beautiful in years to come.

Let's Recap

Recycling is really important to help protect our planet and everything that lives within it.

If we recycle our card and paper, plastics, metals and glass, it means we can turn things that are no longer useful, or rubbish, into new items that can be used again. This can be done again and again and again, instead of being buried in the ground or put into the ocean, where it never goes away.

This could be turning old newspaper into egg boxes. Or making cardboard boxes into new boxes and drinks cans into new cans. Or even bigger changes like making playground equipment from old toys and even carpet from plastic bottles.

Take your time to think about which parts of our rubbish can be recycled and made into new things for us to use. By putting them in the correct bin, we are helping keep the planet clean and safe.

You can make a real difference to our world, if you take time to think about recycling.

Quiz Time

1. What 4 materials do we often recycle?

2. Can you find items made of these four materials throughout the book?

3. Can you think of things in your house that are made from metal, glass, paper and cardboard, and plastic which could be recycled when you have finished using them?

4. Do you know where your recycling bin is at home?

5. Why is it important to recycle?

ACTIVITIES

Can you help to sort the different recyclables into the correct bins?
Draw a line from the rubbish to the bin.

PAPER

PLASTIC

GLASS

METAL

Can you help the girl find her way to the plastic recycling bin?

WORDSEARCH

Can you find the important words about recycling in the grid below?

A	V	S	E	G	L	M	E	T	A	L
F	B	R	U	B	B	I	S	H	Q	A
S	O	X	B	R	N	S	P	V	L	U
A	R	L	C	W	L	G	D	Y	A	S
P	E	X	T	G	L	A	S	S	N	C
L	C	R	H	T	W	C	V	H	D	P
A	Y	E	R	E	U	S	E	I	F	A
S	C	S	A	M	S	O	H	S	I	P
T	L	D	T	H	U	P	E	K	L	E
I	E	L	O	A	V	L	B	S	L	R
C	N	C	A	R	D	B	O	A	R	D

CARDBOARD	GLASS	PLASTIC
LANDFILL	METAL	RECYCLE
RUBBISH	PAPER	REUSE

Answers available at: youandwhattodo.com/answers

Coming soon to the You and What to Do series

Emergencies, You and What To Do
John Cooper

The Seasons, You and What To Do
John Cooper

Keep up to date with the latest releases from the *You and What To Do* series at
www.youandwhattodo.com

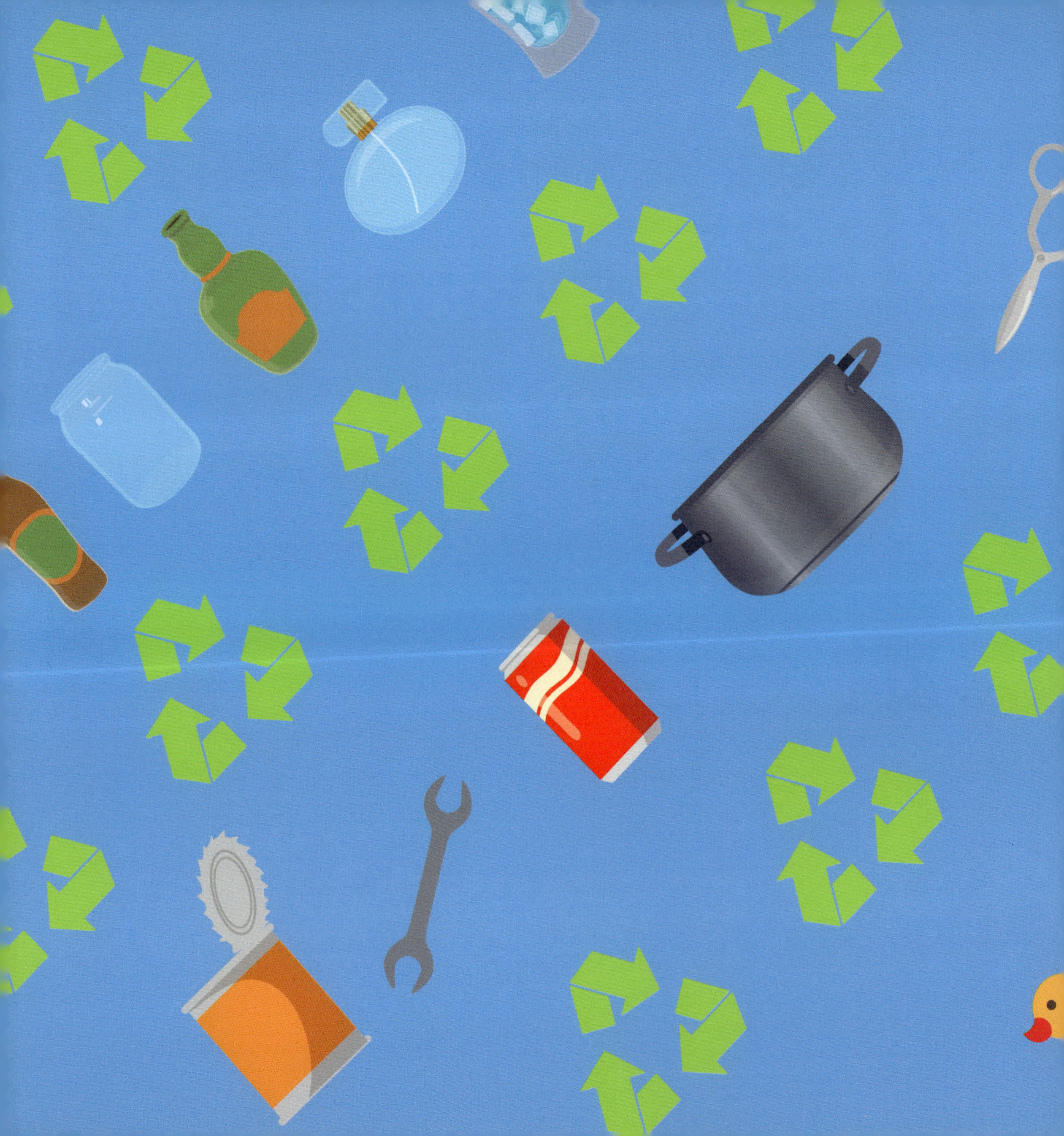

Copyright © 2021

John Cooper

All rights reserved.

No part of this publication may be reproduced, stored in a retrieval system, or transmitted in any form or by any means, electronic, mechanical, photocopying, recording, or otherwise, without written permission from the publisher. For information regarding permission, write to **hello@youandwhattodo.com**

Published in the United Kingdom

Written and designed by John Cooper.

ISBN:

Paperback: 979-8-7744-2498-6

Printed in Great Britain
by Amazon